COME CLOSE AND LISTEN

Jim C. Wilson

August 2018.

COME CLOSE AND LISTEN

JIM C. WILSON

Greenwich Exchange
London

ACKNOWLEDGEMENTS

Thanks to editors of the following publications in which these poems, or versions of them, first appeared: *Acumen, Books In Scotland, Cencrastus, Chapman, "14", Edinburgh: An Intimate City, Gutter, Haiku Scotland, Imago (Australia), New Writing Scotland, No Choice But To Trust (Canada), NorthWords, Northwords Now, Orbis, Outposts, Poetry Scotland, Stand, Understanding, The Dark Horse, The Eildon Tree, The Herald (newspaper), The Rialto.*

Greenwich Exchange, London

First published in Great Britain in 2014
All rights reserved

Come Close and Listen © Jim C. Wilson 2014

Printed and bound by imprintdigital.net
Cover design by December Publications
Tel: 028 90286559

Greenwich Exchange Website: www.greenex.co.uk

Cataloguing in Publication Data is available from the British Library

Cover art: 'A Lady at the Virginal with a Gentleman: The Music Lesson' by Johannes Vermeer
Royal Collection Trust/© Her Majesty Queen Elizabeth II, 2014

ISBN: 978-1-906075-85-9

for Mik, whom I first met in 1967 –
and who still listens to me

'Writing a poem's like opening curtains; first you see more but, as night falls, others can see you.'

– Tim Love

CONTENTS

COME CLOSE AND LISTEN

It seems at times I am sentenced
     to echo endlessly
          inside this skull,

sifting through a cairn
     of inadequate words,
          ambiguous phrases.

Visitors peer inside my eyes
     yet fail to distinguish
          a hint of presence,

while I rehearse responses,
     try out perfect arguments,
          prepare my case yet again.

The specialist thinks I am silent
     but he can't hear the hiss of blood,
          the thudding of each second.

And he doesn't detect me, from midnight
     till noon, as I stack and restack
          my words of gold

to build another absolute poem.
     Sometimes ideas just fall away
          like soft old cobwebs;

and images will suddenly crack
    like dull broken moons.
        But poetry is possible

and often I will sing out loud
    in here, to myself,
        in this hall of bone.

Will you please come close now?
    Listen. Syllables are almost
        on my tongue.

UTTER

A poem is hovering in the southern sky,
its meaning waxing, waning, like the moon.
Its words could touch upon your hair, your mouth;
I just don't know, don't know how it will end,
and shifting cloud might make the substance thin.
All might come clear if only I could sleep.

My syntax cracks, words warp, unless I sleep,
yet when day fades I'm drawn towards that sky,
and stars which punctuate, while light gets thin.
Then I discern the crack across the moon.
I must just trap beginning, middle, end;
feel syllables evolve deep in my mouth.

But an aftertaste like panic fills my mouth
and there's no lullaby to induce sleep.
A single singing line would serve to end
this sense of senselessness. Give me the sky
and bring me, please, the mystique of the moon
for me to make your perfect poem. A thin

insistent voice says no. The air seems thin,
my breathing slight and slow. My open mouth
would swallow down that cold November moon
but miracles don't come, nor soothing sleep.
Your sonnet tells of geese across the sky;
cycles and seasons, the world without end;

right now *my* poem is only glimmers. End-
ing now might stop my patience wearing thin.
I'd turn my back against the darkening sky,
erase all images, then hush my mouth.
Would I then descend into silent sleep?
Could I then resist the pull of the moon?

I have my doubts. And perhaps no choice. Moon-
light pervades this room; I brood on an end,
recall the beginning. There's time for sleep
when the lines are complete, the bone-thin
fingers of dawn draw near. And from my mouth,
my tongue, the words will fill my hungry sky.

You are my moon. When all of life seems thin,
love near an end, let your mouth touch my mouth,
utter the poem, speak the stars, breathe the sky.

SOMONKA

His Approach

This tanka would be
on a fan of rice paper
at plum-blossom time
had I mastered the koto's
thirteen silver silken strings.

Her Response

Before I could pluck
just the sound of their falling
the white camellias
would have blossomed many times,
your tanka unacknowledged.

Response composed by Jane Rodger

NATURALLY

In the botanical garden's
wild flower collection
stonecrop flaunted
its thick fleshy leaves
as meadowsweet moistly
stood by the pool;
saxifrage clung
to the crumbling wall
as gipsywort
bent to the breeze;
bindweed twined
and curled round stems
as marjoram
swayed purple, scented;
nipplewort
displayed in the shade
as honeysuckle
hung from hedges;
and as the sun rose
higher, hotter,
and when no-one
was there to see,
for her he plucked
forget-me-nots.

LEAVETAKING

'I'm not sure if I should be here,' you said,
then talked of bees and popping trees, and love
that came and went like the sea, and would not
let you be what you thought you ought to be.
I'm on the shore now, casting my stones,
watching them skip, splash and sink. But your eyes
are drawn to the other side, and a wind
from the east means you're leaving me soon –
perhaps. A small white feather rides the waves,
carried to and fro as I bluntly wonder
why I'm not enough for you, why you wish
for a life of aloneness and bone. But
your plans are made, your work awaits. You will
journey far into yourself, leaving me poems
and the sound of your laughter. Meanwhile
a leaf still clings to the tree, and I can't
see beyond you as the prettiest nun.

THE TREES SEEM STILL

Sometimes the trees are deadly still:
they stand in streets, in line with walls.
Sometimes they loom like monuments.

Some days I'm lifeless as those trees,
with no sap coursing, no leaves unfurled.
I'm dark against a darkening sky;

and always the thought of the cankered bough,
the slicing saw, then rings exposed:
all life reduced to an inert stump.

But a still tree breathes, a still tree grows,
while cutting patterns over the sun
and reinterpreting the moon.

And a tree will sing in winter wind,
daub blossom on a city spring.
Deepening greens define the summer.

Let me grow on way past autumn,
colouring paths and parks and hills.
Let me eke some poetry from rings.

SOPHIA PLAYS THE PIANO

Look in through the high bow windows,
hear the muffled notes. Sophia sits
as in a frame, her back as straight
as the spine of a book. Pause as her fingers
pick out the years and piece together
bits of the past. Remember the girl
with the flaxen hair, how she ran
through fields of ripening corn. And did
she miss a note there? Her fingers
freeze; she's still. She's still. See her lips
begin to move. But it's just old words
you cannot hear. A beam of sun
cuts through a cloud and hits against
the window glass; it lightens the varnish
in the room. Sophia adjusts
a velvet sleeve; then her fingers
explore the empty paths, go through
the gardens in the rain. The sunlight fades,
her fingers walk, they're making tracks
in December snow. See Sophia,
she's stepping out, down through the valley,
towards the woods. Her face is bright. She laughs.
See her dancing like the snowflakes;
watch her melting into spring.

THEIR GARDEN

Late autumn, yet the stream is just a trickle.
A mass of crows is watching from the oak
while, muffled in old clothes, he tidies leaves.
She's inside, reading, thinking of abroad –
and how the airport's now impossible.
Funny how the hours and years get shorter
and yet that sky grows bigger every day.
They'd planned to change the place, adapt, convert,
but now the bathroom window glass stays cracked.
The evergreen they planted years ago
had seemed a kind of symbol of their love.
One winter it had withered, nearly died.
'A subject for a poem, perhaps,' he thinks,
as weakening sunlight filters through the branches,
disappears, and leaves him wondering in the shade.

PRUNING

I dock the dead, the damaged and diseased;
the gnarled and dry come tumbling from the heights
until I stand knee-deep in bits, well-pleased
I've put a few square yards of world to rights.
I clip and crop, encouraging new growth.
My fingers start to ache but still I snap
my Homebase secateurs. I grin as both
the gleaming silver blades expose more sap.
I deftly make the kindest cuts, and take
the part of surgeon, Adam, God. But mend
myself, I cannot. No sharp shears will make
me sprout, or slow my geriatric trend.
So, wrinkling, stiffening, stooping, short of breath,
I spend my weekends saving plants from death.

SUZANNE ET GÉRARD À *LA JARISSIE*

'Of course, we're hard at work throughout the day:
I've got the dogs to walk. And brush. It's *such*
a handful, running this big place. I lay
the breakfast table. Then it's lunch; not much:
an omelette, dry white wine. And then I feed
the dogs and take the cover off the pool.
I might just have a dip, or sit and read
through letters, papers. Gérard, as a rule,
does heavy work. Right now he's in his den,
tying flies for fishing. He likes to mow
the grass, on his little tractor thing. Men!
Life's lovely, really, but it *is* all go.'
Suzanne is staring at her woods, her park;
so *very* much to do before the dark.

RETIRED

Damned hot again today. Must have a gin,
then check the stocks and shares while Daisy gets
her hair and nails done. There's quite a lot
to do today, in truth. The pears are ripe,
too ripe, almost (work there for the gardener).
The club, Cedric says, has got a new chef:
Brown Windsor, Gammon Steak and Sunday Roast.
We'll have to check that out; early days, though, yet.
I'll drive to town this afternoon, perhaps;
drop into The Bull for a chinwag,
or watch the golf – a boon that cable set-up.
And the pool could do with a bit of a clean.
So glad we upped our roots and got away.
Life's great. But, God, the Costa's hot today.

FAMILY

The children have gone, so now Mum and Dad
can do just what they choose. They lie in late
then eat breakfast slowly, as though they had
all the time in the world. As sure as fate,

Dad will relax for a couple of hours
with his paper. Then he and Mum will take
the ten-to-twelve bus to Tesco. 'Flowers,
Love?' he sometimes asks, knowing that she'll shake

her head and say they have a gardenful.
Some photos came from Pete in Winnipeg.
'Done well, our kids,' said Dad. 'Kate with a pool,
three cars.' And he thought of his numb right leg.

They went on a tour – to cheer themselves up.
When the bus stopped at York, they had hot pies
with crinkle-cut chips on the side; a cup
of tea to end, as a tape played 'Spanish Eyes'.

Back on the bus Dad fell asleep, while Mum
stared out at traffic. 'I think we've got old,'
she thought, and wondered when the kids would come.
Dad sat up quick; he said his feet felt cold.

MR & MRS MURDOCH GO CYCLING

Mr and Mrs Murdoch sat firm astride
their racing bikes for over fifty years.
They had a baby once, taught him to ride
behind them, his hat down over his ears.

They pedalled forever through sun and snow,
cycling to Thurso, back down to Dunoon.
(In shorts, with capes and canvas bags, they'd go,
I'm sure, and light their Primus on the moon –

if they had the relevant map.) But years
began to overtake them; motorways
sliced through their quiet lanes. Yet, changing gears,
the Murdochs pedalled on through shortening days

until, in the end, they slackened their pace.
They got off to rest from a long, slow climb
and a passing tractor removed his face.
It was shortly before the harvest time.

IN MILNE'S BAR

The old man sits with his back to the wall;
staring and crinkled, he grips
his pint of light,
his hand dry as dead heather.
He sees a stranger, a girl
across the smoky room.
She smiles.
The old man fingers the ashtray.
His night gets longer
until a blackbird starts to sing.
His young bride beckons
from over a stream.
He almost gets up to go.

THE HUNCHBACK AT THE BAR

Hunch? Hump? He's sure it's more a curve,
a rise. And with his roomy anorak, well,
who would ever notice? Another large gin,
and half-smile for the barmaid; big girl,
she is, and him only four-feet-eleven.
And her jeans are so tight that's he's sure
they must hurt. He averts his eyes,
and fingers his tie. Perfect, in the mirror.
The loud boys barge past but he never stirs –
or complains – it's good just to be there,
mixing with folk. He likes to hear the chat,
the deals, the arguments and laughter. Sometimes
he nods or shakes his head, takes a point of view.
His shoes almost sparkle; his suit is neat,
it's made-to-measure. He bathes twice a day
(at least), meaning to make the best impression.
Some night he'll talk with a willowy girl,
inhale the scent of her new-washed hair.
He'll stare into her confident eyes, escort
her back to his immaculate flat –
then enfolding him close with her long lithe arms,
she'll not even notice his hump, the curve.
Sweat glows on his forehead, 'Excuse me, Miss.'
Has he got time for one last large gin?

THE VISITOR

Gravestones lie flat; abandoned casualties.
The tall wet grass moves over them.
A finger traces names in the moss,
finding out if they've faded yet.

The visitor has skin like paper,
dry-twig bones, and hair like snow.
She looks for paths, she pokes for clues
among the broken flowers and urns.

The grass gathers all into the ground,
covering births and names and deaths,
and deep in a handbag, deep in a purse,
a baby smiles through Cellophane.

Caught in a snare of clinging weed,
the graveyard gates no longer move;
and the visitor can't quite squeeze through
to where the children play in the sun.

She hears their voices, hears their laughter;
she reaches out her hand to them.
The sunlight flashes on her ring
and a little boy plays dead in the grass.

FLOWERING LATE

She was in her autumn when he came, bear-
ing love, and a yucca plant. It stood guard
at her bedroom window; the panicles,
seedful and pendent, quivered. It was hard

for her to ignore the burst of long leaves,
that fountain of green; had it been a child
or a grave it would not have been better
tended. That yucca entirely beguiled

and involved her and yet it did not flower
until, years after, some soft lilacious
blooms broke out, hanging like snow on the green
daggers. And again she grew vivacious,

knew a pang of warmth, remembering how
his love took root when she believed her fate
was to pass her quiet years in brittle
endurance; then at last it flowered, late.

THREE TANKA CONCERNING LOSS

On this grey March day
wondering about a cup
of coffee and you
I notice the place we met
is boarded up and for sale.

Before the mists clear
I am at your locked front door
holding half a poem.
As I wait, it's spring again.
Again the blossom, the words.

This year the berries
on the holly appear
more red than ever.
So many – so many months
since opening your last letter.

WHAT'S LEFT

The glass
you drank from sits
amongst the napkins, crumbs.
I see the prints of your fingers
and lips.

BARRIERS

In Glasgow's Winter Garden
incessant rain leaks through the roof.

Long drops splutter on paving-stones.
An iron table separates

the couple. They're silent, chilled.
Her lips are moving with emotion;

uncertain. Has he said too much?
His hand edges towards her,

across the crumbs and crumpled napkins.
She retreats into her overcoat.

Above, two blackbirds try to reach
each other. She's inside, imprisoned;

he's out in the rain, frantic, scrabbling,
throwing himself against the glass

and terrified he's being abandoned.

ON EXMOOR

One more shower of rain;
one more wash of sunlight
across that shaven hillscape.
The wind pulled at our bones
and the path we took
was split by a spine of grass.

The pastures were swollen
with burial mounds;
one more buzzard cut the sky.
You followed me, your scarf wound tight
against the chill. Berries shone out
at us like blood.

And round the corner
the horse and rider barred my way;
across my path, and high as trees.
I waited for your company,
was waiting in the late October dusk
as the land fell away to the sea.

UNSEEN

These woods
look empty but
echo with sudden hints
and sighs; in the unstirring air
there's you.

I NEED TO HOLD YOU NOW

The ten-year kitchen noise of squawks and chirps
and witterings has stopped; our house has lost
its accompaniment. This morning heard
me whistling at the air, its emptiness.

He had a lump, was growing short of breath,
and yet we hoped he'd sing until forever.
We never thought he'd push into your puzzle book
and, soft and bright as always, lie still.

He sang his song when my brother died. He
sang out when my mother died, was singing
when your father died. Those absences
are back again; I feel them in our rooms.

Last night we wrapped our bird in cloth,
buried him near the river. We slipped in mud,
we didn't say much. I need to hold you now.
I see his claws; they're closing on thin air.

FIRST WINTER AFTER FLITTING

Bright berries on the cotoneaster
cluster red in persistent bunches.

Dead leaves dropped by the holly tree
draw shining beads of blood from my hands.

The robin is always searching alone;
his fire's a darting gleam in the frost.

Each colder morning the doves are here;
just two of them, in the thinning dark.

And this someone-else's house we're in:
will the spring make it grow less strange?

CHANCE

How many playing-cards will I be dealt?
(Hear them tick-ticking onto my table.)
One for every season of each of seventy
years? Or will my body tire of the game?

And will the red be outnumbered by black?
I fear they will, but who am I to judge?
But then my Queen of Hearts is shining still.
Diamonds or dust; she's still here with me.

The cards keep coming, though less and less aces;
faster and fainter they flick past my eyes.
The final one could be colourless, limp –
or brighter than sunrise, crisper than stars.

LAST NIGHT

Last night in bed
your breathing sounded
oddly like the chiming
of a distant clock;
not digital
or electronic –
more like the one
in my parents' house,
which ticked and slowed,
forever losing minutes.
So what could I do
but listen and listen
as night turned slowly
towards the dawn?

NIGHTLINES

Listen to the night,
its unseen insects;
and suddenly
the owl's voice,
its warning so ancient,
so true,
that even the moon
appears
to listen.

DREAMLANDS

Your breathing is irregular.

Are you hearing again
your father's lorry wheels
scrunching deep into the gravel?
Are you waving goodbye
to your mother again,
leaving so early, riding
her bike to the marshes?
Are you drowning a little
as I stand nearby
and heartlessly watch
– as I usually do?

All these, perhaps, while I lie
here guessing, wondering
where on this earth you can be,
until once more I climb
those stairs and take my place
on the shining linoleum,
switch on the old wireless,
and wait, wait, wait
for a kind of fun to begin.

AT SEA

As he slips deeper into sleep
he's swimming in the silver waves
and sees in the east
the cliffs become gull-white
in the light of a rising moon;
he recalls the soft salt flesh
of mussels and how in waves
they open.
            Then his eyes unseal
in a room that is silent
and the cold colour of ivory;
he senses again the absence
that looms like a leviathan.

THE BEASTS

The colourless slugs come out at night;
they range beyond my closed doors,
graze, with all the time in the world,
on pieces of unpleasantness and moss.
I would not squeeze their moist softness,
even for riches beyond my dreams.

The beasts slide through my nights, horns waving.
I wake each day and face their tangled trails.

THE LAST TRAM

The last tram is white; here it comes now,
slipping silently along its tracks of steel.
See the passengers. Why don't they wave?
Their eyes all look towards the driver. He's

in control, knows when to ring the bell.
The back of the tram looks like the front:
so will it stop, return to the depot?
No, it just glides along its tracks, further,

further down the road, leaving me to stand
and wait. I watch it go; I watch
with my late father. He grips my hand,
at least for a while. Then he too is gone.

The last tram finally leaves the road
and skims across the bright green grass.
The conductor laughs; the passengers smile;
I enjoy the view from the windows at last.

THE HIDDEN PLACE

Who can live beyond that yellow door?
It stands so neat and so intact
in its flawless whitewashed wall.

An overhanging branch with lemons
cuts across the dead-straight frame
and makes the scene a composition.

I try to imagine the other side
as I stretch to pluck the imperfect fruit,
then squeeze myself a cool, bitter drink

to sip in the shade while I contemplate
if it's love or fear that keeps me here,
this side of that shining yellow door.

LIFE LOOKED OUT

Life looked out from a broken door;
she promised everything to me.
'Come on in, there's time to kill.
Come in, there's all to see.'

I could not go into that place;
all in the house seemed dead.
I turned away from Life's pale eyes.
'Just passing through,' I said.

LOCKED WARD

I'm pregnant again.
They won't believe me when I tell them;
won't even let me pick fresh flowers.

I'll need to knit
more christening shawls – as soon
as they take me down to the bathroom.

The water in these flowers
is yellow – and me in my condition!
Soon it'll be the funny cravings.

Remember the time
I tucked into lipstick, got red
all up my nicest nightie?

John'll be thrilled
to hear the news; he'll visit me tonight;
he always comes when I've had my jag.

Oh, but I'm big!
They want me to keep my nightie down
but they must be told about baby.

I'll pick new lilies for the cradle
when I get my clothes. And here comes baby,
warm and wet, filling the bed with love.

TWO CINQUAINS FOR THE END OF DECEMBER

Midwinter

Across
thin ice again;
the firs rigid with frost.
What unseen bird calls, unearthly,
distant?

About To Leave

The house
is dark, as is
the road; and I can't scrape
the windscreen ice away. It is
so cold.

INFECTION

It seems that all the world's asleep, except
for me. It's after three, my raw nose streams,
the rafters echo with my clammy cough. Kept
awake, I curse all those who drift in dreams.
So out of bed and down the hall I creep.
My perspiration chills; my jacket clings.
The kitchen seems not right, its quietness deep:
a lethargy contaminates all things.
Then pills, hot juice – and the ghosts come calling.
They sit through the night; they're frightened, they're thin.
Most come from the past, frail, almost falling;
some come from the future, sure to get in.
And I, at this time of least resistance,
look to lighted windows in the distance.

YOUR CLASSICAL STATION
FOR GENTLE SEDATION

Relax with Rachmaninov
then chill with Tchaikovsky;
sleep it off with Smooth Classics
at Seven.
Just email or text us,
say something inane;
we'll transport you to digital
heaven.

There's ads for investments
and bargain insurance
interspersed with soft music
that calms:
an extract from Elgar,
a snippet of Tippett
and that old, sleepy, slow thing
by Brahms.

You can doze to Debussy,
pass out to Purcell,
hear Lloyd Webber and Liszt
interwoven.
We've classics collated
for easy consumption –
curl up with our background
Beethoven.

We've cantatas, sonatas
and sumptuous CDs
made for lovers and babies
and Mum;
soak up some Sibelius,
stretch out with some Strauss –
just switch off your brain
and succumb!

HOW CATHERINE THE GREAT RELAXED

At an exhibition of the treasures of Catherine the Great, probably the richest and most powerful woman of her time, a notice stated that her favourite pastime was making imitation jewels out of papier-mâché

The Prussian princess, Sophie Auguste,
moved up in the world and changed her name:
Yekaterina (that's Catherine to us)
seemed seemly – that's who she became.
And after she'd collared the clergy's cash
and replenished old Russia's coffers,
and after she'd seen off Peter the Third –
her husband, then critics and scoffers,
and after she'd romped with twenty lovers
(despite being decidedly plain),
and after she'd multiplied numbers of serfs
and made slaves of half the Ukraine,
and after inviting Voltaire for tea,
buying thousands of art works and gowns,
and after splitting Poland apart
and constructing a hundred new towns,
and after fighting and beating the Turks
and expanding both southwards and west,
she added 200,000 square miles
to what she already possessed,
and after revising the system of law
she dashed off a book or two;
but sometimes she wearied, had to unwind,
she'd enough of do, do, do;
but she didn't knit or play balalaika,

make arrangements of petals and stems:
Cath fashioned papier-mâché
into artificial gems.

SOME NAMES

Some names fit perfectly in verse; they sound
so right: like Leda. (You need a gripping
story too. Like how, when strolling around
a pond, she encountered a swan, just dripping
with lust. And, as Yeats tells it, the bird had
its way, feathers flew – then the poor girl laid
two eggs.) Cynara stars in a sad, sad
poem, by sadder Ernest Dowson. Made
him weep, the sweet girl did, but he stayed true
in his fashion. Then there's Aphrodite,
Juliet; Maud and Mariana: they, too,
have been immortalised, whether flighty
or devoted. Some are chaste, some are racy,
but never called Senga, Sal or Tracy.

AFTER THE READINGS

Fine words are spoken on friendship and love
then the poets retire to the bar; pints
appear and, in the gloom, the whole wide world
is put to rights (at least in their own minds).
That bastard's been bought up by Bloodaxe Books
and so-and-so's new volume is vile! Yes, sonnets
are back, the money's no good, and should
they have just one more drink? And *The Scotsman*,
they're sure, has gone down the pan; yes, peanuts
are fine, how's your glass? And as the clock ticks
on and on, a woman sits and stares. 'See
you,' she cries, Greek-chorus-like: 'You all talk shit.'
It's late and it's cold, there are hills to climb;
through moonlit streets, the poets sway, in time.

UNLIKELY COMPANIONS

Englyn For Emily

Your soul alone at night – a ticking clock.
Death comes close, his smile bright.
Eyes reflect the cool lamplight.
Then, in neat quatrains, you write.

Dylan Thomas (38)

He slowly recounts sheep (his tongue has dried)
then sweats in chains of sleep;
laughing maidens primp and peep
while the dew-drenched apples seep.

WESTMINSTER BRIDGE REVISITED

As, William, you are here today with me,
will you buy a burger from that stall, while
dodging teeming trails of tourists? You see
the Thames, grey-green and deep, and you can smile
as you recall that splendid silent dawn
in a time when cities *slept* at night. Hills
and fields? You won't see them. And you might yawn
as you survey our bland satanic mills:
Shell-Mex and a thousand others. But look!
To our right! Glittering, bright: a mighty wheel
we call the London Eye. In your next book
you could include a view seen from the sky. We'll
get two tickets quick and, once we're on it,
William, I suggest you write a sonnet.

THE POET WHO WROTE OF MOTHS

She was
quick and silent,
never seeming
to enter a room.
And on the stroke
of an invisible clock
she vanished
as she'd come.

1936

Oh Lorca, did skeletons show
gold teeth to you

when men held you down
in their terrible passion,

thrust the rifle deep in your bowels,
fired into your intestines?

Or did you recall the balcony
opening to the summer mountains,

and see the boy suck oranges
as the harvester cut down the corn?

And could you taste a sailor's kiss
in that black grove of olives?

Before the last explosion of blood,
did you remember love?

THE CAMP

Why so many broken, wooden feet? Why
so many yellowed straps and rusted buckles,
metal corsets, arms with levers, cracked thighs?
Two rigid hands reach out, as if to hug.
Why so many pairs of glasses, sightless
things with shattered lenses? The thin wire frames
are bent and twisted, intermingled, piled
up high. (Spectators, we all stand and stare.)
And now the hair. One whole roomful, lifeless,
dry. Back then it was measured in sacks, in tons,
went straight from shorn scalps to assembly lines.
Hour after hour, year after year – the cutting.
Old combs and toys and heaps of empty cases:
so much to see, because there were so many.

NOWHERE

I try to sleep,
to dream of my family
but the gate crashes open,
the hood goes on again.

Backwards down some corridor
into a room
to kneel again.

It's the short shackles now –
twenty minutes, twenty hours,
with my head down,
bowing,
shaved.

Again the shouting
and the touching.
I try to please
but the headphones are ready,
slip over my ears.

There's a cold wind
round my body now
and the noise is back
in my bones, in my soul –
louder than sirens, jet planes,
bombs.

White and endless,
utterly endless.

And now my scalp
is starting to peel.

IN THE TORTURE MUSEUM, AMSTERDAM

A few euros each, and we join the queue
to stand before the prize acquisition.
Something's not right yet we jostle to view
the souvenir of the Inquisition.

In pride of place, a chair, its timber dark
and unrelenting. Like an empty throne
or judgement seat, this chair stands stark,
and chill as stone; its silence speaks of bone.

And the nails, the nails, their long iron points.
They rise in neat rows from arms, seat and back,
slid swiftly through skin, to muscles and joints.
(Details are briefly described on a plaque.)

The body's own weight was all that it took:
no need for pressure or giving a hand.
The questioners waited, had a good look,
then soaked up the mess with sackcloth or sand.

But those men with their piercing chair of pain,
their wheels, their racks and crippling cages, could
not compete with the One they served. His reign
was absolute, supreme. He had no crude

machines or clamps. And when you're judge and lord
of all, you don't have to press for answers:
just sit on high with a glittering sword,
dispensing your famines, plagues and cancers.

In pride of place, the chair of nails. It tells
of hell on earth, and shows what man can do
to man. And it speaks to me of the hells
gods send, when every point will go clean through.

SO CLOSE

The pink house grins through a death mask of mist;
in the cellar another tooth is snapped.

A husband dreams blood, his face to the wall;
silk fibres get trapped by his fingernails.

The tramp in the doorway lies motionless;
the beggar's lean dogs are waltzing slowly.

Softly, young mums nurse flowerlike bruises;
are rarely seen without their dark glasses.

Children are cursing the price of cocaine;
one more last drink's alright for the road.

The News is oozing with underwear tales.
His hard disk holds photos of girls and boys.

Getting so close to the ladder's last rung;
recalling the dark of March, how it clung.

VINCENT EXERCISING (1890)

I see myself:
I follow the man in front,
am followed by the man behind,
circling like the hands of a clock,
from midnight to noon,
noon until midnight.
The brick walls reach up heavenwards
and I cannot see a door.

But I will walk free –
in the room
where rhythms are all my own
and the sunflowers glow
having swallowed the sun
in field after field –
on wall after wall after wall.

TINDERBOX

Just in case his hotel caught fire
Hans Christian Andersen carried a rope,
his means of escape from the nightmare pyre
if, sometime soon, his hotel caught fire.
Each day he expected something dire
(though snow queens and mermaids helped him cope).
So, just in case his hotel caught fire
Hans Christian Andersen carried a rope.

ON 57TH STREET
'Nighthawks', Edward Hopper, 1942

And if I call her, she just might say no
or put me off with some excuse or tale
of other obligations, so I'll just show
her I don't care, sit here at the bar, pale
and hunched, like Bogart or Sinatra, cool
as the night, yet hot for action. I'll get
another shot of Scotch – though, boy, this stool
is hard, and I haven't moved since six. Bet
the bartender thinks I'm a lush, but he
knows nothing, the jumped-up punk, and that dame
in the fur ain't no Betty Grable. She
sits there, she's posing, as though in a frame.

Damn jukebox only plays one song, 'Blue Moon'.
One drink, and then I guess I'll call her, soon.

DUETS
'The Music Lesson' (1665) by Johannes Vermeer

Listen, I'll put you in the picture: she
and I have made sweet music; in fact I taught
her all she knows. But now she plays while he
stands near; he's hunting and I fear she's caught.
The keys are touched by her fingertips; I hear
the melody she played for me, can almost see
him by the virginal, so poised, his leer
suppressed, dark staff in hand, sword hanging free.
What use is music now, except as balm
for sorrow? Should I have leaned a little
closer, risked familiarity? Am
I the one who broke what was so brittle?
My untuned viol and bow lie on the floor,
beyond my reach, inside her closing door.

CHET BAKER'S DENTURES

Your dentures never fitted, quite,
and trumpeters *must* have their teeth:
constant trouble with your embouchure.

And then there was the heroin
and other stuff you used for years
while your dentures never fitted, quite.

Your audience would wait for hours
as you fixed yourself and your dental plate:
constant trouble with your embouchure.

But then you'd blow some silver notes:
sparse, and cool as an April moon.
And your dentures never fitting, quite.

When playing got tough you'd sing
like a girl, to ease your lips, your tongue;
constant trouble with your embouchure.

Your not-quite disembodied voice
sang 'Long Ago And Far Away',
while your dentures never fitted, quite.

One night in Amsterdam you slipped;
like Icarus you failed to fly,
ending trouble with your embouchure.

We have the soundtrack of your life:
restless, searching, incomplete,
when your dentures never fitted, quite;
constant trouble with your embouchure.

J.W. LENNON, 1957

This boy imagines he might be The King
while digging for rock with his Quarrymen.
Then 'Bring a little water, Sylvie,' he sings
in the cottonfields of his aunt's back kitchen.
Three chords later, there's that boy Paul, and praise
for pretty Peggy Sue. There's nylon strings
and nylon stockings; time to strum and wake
up Susie. This boy can now do anything:
even walk the streets in blue suede shoes
and a black leather jacket like Be-bop Gene's.
The Light Programme is playing light music
but John has learned all the words of 'Lucille'.
He's going to Kansas City, the USA;
across the universe, yeah, all the way.

ARABESQUE

The sultan does not move:
he stares beyond the cypresses;
he sees the snows of spring
unmelted on the sharp sierras.

The July scents of myrtle,
rose and jasmine do not delight
the sultan now; he sits
straightbacked on his bench of stone,

while she, supple as young wands
of willow, dances in the Hall
of Sisters, hearing the songs
of ten thousand fountains.

Moorish curves of wood and plaster
mimic the enraptured girl who whirls
and bends and sways. Her bare feet
are kissed by the cool blue tiles,

while the sultan observes
the thin crescent moon; it rises
slowly, beyond the peaks.
He sees the trembling of the stars.

KARDAMILI

Beyond
the stars, more stars;
light on the night water;
then, unanimous, cicadas,
silent.

AT THE BEACH

On a beach as long as the moon is bleak
she sees dunes climb, until their jagged grasses
stab the sky. And the message is *Don't Run,*
Don't Play, Don't Even Attempt To Touch. The sand's
as golden as Teddy's fur, but the softness
that she loves to sift, feel between her toes,
is littered, bulging, broken. Barbed wire curls,
it writhes in twisting spirals. There to tear
flesh, in and out it snakes its cold steel way.
Concrete steps lead up to nowhere, leaning;
and, in dead clumps, red bricks cling together.
It's said there are unexploded things; they
just might blast a limb away. So best to stand
by the cold water's edge, where coal creeps in
on the evening tide and sleek seagulls scream.
'A bad beach,' she says and grabs Daddy's hand.
They follow the crescent bay in silence,
towards the far power station. It sits
at the point that's known as The Scars, and looks
as small as a doll's house; its hum is lost
in the sighs of the wind. Breezes finger
her shining hair, as shifting sand drifts up
the beach but fails to cover the remains,
the hellish junk and testament of war.
The North Sea darkens. A man in a coat
is picking up coal. 'We'll come back and play
in the spring,' she says. And a plane flies low,
silver reflecting a last glance of sun.

WORDS FOR AN UNKNOWN ADAGIO

Must I set sail on a marble sea
where air hangs dead as ash, and no winds
breathe? I have no wish to cross that grey
and motionless tract, yet know,
out there, a silent island waits,
its black cliffs taller than cathedral walls.

The boatman stands; he'd stand forever,
his gaze so steady and relentless.
'You'll pay me when it's time to go,'
his voice as soft as melting candlewax.

A night bird cries; the sound is darker
than starless skies in winter.
The tide is turning but I stay still,
surrounded by limp fingers of weed,
and boulders lying like stranded beasts.

The boatman smiles as he enfolds me
deep inside his colourless cloak,
and it's almost time to hear the music.

Across the water, the cellist waits –
her bow about to strike the strings.

A YEAR

Swifts screech past windows;
they've come from nowhere, sudden
as the warmth on walls.

An aeroplane hums
through the blue, as far away
as a child's summer.

Dry leaves like cracked tongues
hang in autumn smoke; the wind
tells bedtime stories.

In December hours
of darkness, a sudden star
through tangled branches.

THE END OF WAITING

Every hour now I awake and reach
to clutch the wartime stocking,
limp white netting with a frayed red trim.

What if again I've been left out?
I watch the paper blind for shadows;
was that the creak of a boot in the hall?

Here in the dark, with nothing new to touch
or stroke, I live my sins once more,
fingering the empty stocking's length,

until, and it is all of a sudden,
the netting's stretched, the leg is bulging.
I feel lumps, and Santa's been at last.

SELECTED POETRY TITLES
from GREENWICH EXCHANGE

FIRST LIGHT & OTHER POEMS
Warren Hope

£9.99 (pbk)
978-1-906075-80-4 60pp

Warren Hope's poetry is firmly grounded in reality. A lyricist of the everyday, Hope recognises and captures in words the small transformative moments of living. The poems of First Light are those of a poetic craftsman, one fully at ease with his chosen discipline. At its finest, his work straddles the vibrant vernacular of the United States and the formality of the traditional lyric. The tension between these two idioms – and Hope's reaction to it – produces a satisfying and challenging collection.

A CHANGE OF SEASON
Michael Cullup

£9.95 (pbk)
978-1-906075-38-5 98pp

In a *TLS* review of *Reading Geographies*, Dick Davis said that Cullup's poems had a 'curmudgeonly, undeceived, deliberate lack of resonance' about them. To C.H. Sisson, they were 'the actual off-scourings of life, which is what I look for'.

A Change of Season is Cullup's first major collection for over a decade and sees the poet at his most assured. Never shying from the great themes - love, loss, mortality - Cullup remains true to a personal vision which haunts and disturbs.

HUNTS: POEMS 1979-2009
John Greening

£7.99 (pbk)
978-1-906075-33-0 262 pp

Hunts: Poems 1979-2009 gathers together highlights from Greening's eleven books along with about sixty new or uncollected poems.

THE LAST BLACKBIRD & OTHER POEMS
Ralph Hodgson

£7.95 (pbk)
978-1-871551-81-5 68pp

Ralph Hodgson (1871-1962) was a poet and illustrator whose most influential and enduring work appeared to great acclaim just prior to, and during, the First World War.

Though never fashionable, his status among poets down the years has grown. Admired by Eliot, Berryman, Spender and Cummings, his work continues to draw praise from contemporary writers.

This new selection brings together, for the first time in 40 years, some of the most beautiful and powerful 'hymns to life' in the English language.

ADAM'S THOUGHTS IN WINTER
Warren Hope

£4.99 (pbk)
ISBN: 978-1-871551-40-2 46pp

Warren Hope's poems have appeared in a number of literary periodicals, pamphlets and anthologies on both sides of the Atlantic. The poems gathered in this first book-length collection counter the brutalising ethos of contemporary life, speaking of, and for, the virtues of modesty, honesty and gentleness in an individual and memorable way.

WONDERING ABOUT MANY WOMEN
Derwent May

£7.99 (pbk)
978-1-906075-62-0 46pp

Gathering together poems written over a number of years, Derwent May's *Wondering About Many Women* enchants not just with its freshness and candour, but also with its distinctive modernity.

Wondering About Many Women is an exuberant demonstration of the power of poetry.

PAPERS
Hollie McNish

£11.95 (pbk)
978-1-906075-67-5 76pp

Hollie McNish's poetry moves with the rhythms, the excitements and disappointments of contemporary life.

Writing more often than not in the intensity of the moment, McNish views our world aslant to produce sometimes startling, sometimes uncomfortable truths.

Already with a devoted following of fans from her poetry readings and performances, Hollie McNish gathers together the best of her work to date in this book.

LIPSTICK
Maggie Butt

£7.99 (pbk)
978-1-871551-94-5 72pp

Lipstick is Maggie Butt's first full collection and marks the entrance of a voice at once witty and wise, poignant and pertinent.

AN ALMOST DANCER
Robert Nye

£7.99 (pbk)
978-1-906075-39-2 58pp

An Almost Dancer sees Robert Nye return to the universal lyric themes of love, loss and mortality. But, as with all true poets, it is the craftsmanship that he brings to his subjects which lifts this collection out of the ordinary and the quotidian. It includes some of Nye's finest work to date.

THE RAIN AND THE GLASS
Robert Nye

£6.99 (pbk)
ISBN: 978-1-871551-41-9 132pp

The Rain and the Glass contains all the poems Nye has written since his *Collected Poems* of 1995, together with his own selection from that volume.

SCRYING STONE
Steven O'Brien

£7.99 (pbk)
ISBN: 978-1-906075-56-9 70pp

Steven O'Brien's poetry, like the geology of his imaginative landscapes, is shot through with the vital ores of language.

Above all, *Scrying Stone* tingles with the joy of words, how they contain the mythic and the magical to inform, infuse and transform the mundane.

THE FLAMING
Marnie Pomeroy

£7.99 (pbk)
ISBN: 978-1-906075-43-9 80pp

Always lyrical and with an assured touch, these poems are remarkable for their range. While some acknowledge raw emotion, others show an underlay of humour. Throughout, an imaginative sensibility shapes what is lovely and speaks through the strange or terrifying. This engaging collection celebrates the value of poetry that can open so many interior landscapes and dialogues with the reader.

COLLECTED POEMS 1943-1993
Martin Seymour-Smith

£9.99 (pbk)
ISBN: 978-1-87551-47-1 184pp

To the general public Martin Seymour-Smith (1928-1998) is known as a distinguished literary biographer, notably of Robert Graves, Rudyard Kipling and Thomas Hardy. But he was, first and foremost, a poet. In this first collected edition of his verse since his death, Martin Seymour-Smith's affinities with the poets of the 17th century becomes clear. He shares their love of argument, ratiocination and a constant wrestling with the self. As this collection, edited by Peter Davies, demonstrates, at the centre of the poems is a passionate engagement with Man, his sexuality and his personal relationships.

WILDERNESS
Martin Seymour-Smith

£4.99 (pbk)
978-1-871551-08-2 52pp

This collection of thirty-six poems is a fearless account of an inner life of love, frustration, guilt, laughter and the celebration of others.

NO THROUGH ROAD
David Sutton

£9.99 (pbk)
ISBN: 978-1-906075-77-4 48pp

His first collection since the well-received *New and Selected Poems 1965-2005*, *No Through Road* sees the poet returning to his chosen territory of the quotidian where real things – love, loss, regret, age, sickness and death – happen. A poet of landscape, Sutton's lyricism also embraces passionately the modern world as we know it.

FLUTTERING HANDS
Stephen Wilson

£7.95 (pbk)
ISBN: 978-1-906075-19-4 80pp

Stephen Wilson's *Fluttering Hands* marks the debut of a lyric poet who combines a romantic sensibility with a restrained, ironic outlook on the human condition. Several poems in this collection are set in Wales where the author has a home, others reflect his Anglo-Jewish identity and ancestry in Eastern Europe.

To find out more about these and other titles visit
www.greenex.co.uk